CONTENTS

Hello World Program

Calculate Sum of Two Numbers

Check Even or Odd Number

Find Factorial of a Number

Check Prime Number

Reverse a String

Count Number of Words in a String

Palindrome Check

Generate Fibonacci Series

Find Largest Number in an Array

Find Smallest Number in an Array

Bubble Sort Algorithm

Insertion Sort Algorithm

Selection Sort Algorithm

Linear Search in an Array

Binary Search Algorithm

Calculate Simple Interest

Calculate Compound Interest

Generate Multiplication Table

Calculate Factorial Using Recursion

Find GCD (Greatest Common Divisor)

Find LCM (Least Common Multiple)

Check Leap Year

Generate Random Numbers

Generate Random Password

Calculate Area of a Circle

Calculate Area of a Triangle

Calculate Area of a Rectangle

Calculate Area of a Square

Calculate Area of a Rhombus

Calculate Area of a Trapezium

Calculate Volume of a Sphere

Calculate Volume of a Cone

Calculate Volume of a Cylinder

Calculate Volume of a Cuboid

Convert Celsius to Fahrenheit

Convert Fahrenheit to Celsius

Convert Kilometers to Miles

Convert Miles to Kilometers

Convert Decimal to Binary

Convert Binary to Decimal

Convert Decimal to Octal

Convert Octal to Decimal

Convert Decimal to Hexadecimal

Convert Hexadecimal to Decimal

Generate a Simple Calculator

Check Armstrong Number

Check Perfect Number

Display ASCII Value of a Character

Generate a Calendar for a Month

Find Roots of a Quadratic Equation

Implement Stack using Array

Implement Queue using Array

Implement Singly Linked List

Implement Doubly Linked List

Implement Circular Linked List

Implement Binary Search Tree (BST)

Implement Insertion Sort Algorithm

Implement Merge Sort Algorithm

Implement Quick Sort Algorithm

Generate Pascal's Triangle

Validate Email Address

Send Email using PHP

Create Login System

Create Registration Form
File Upload and Validation
File Download Script
Create Simple CMS (Content Management System)
Generate XML File using PHP
Parse XML File using PHP
Create JSON Response using PHP
Parse JSON Data using PHP
Implement CRUD Operations (Create, Read, Update, Delete)
Generate Captcha Image
Implement Image Upload and Resize
Generate Thumbnails of Images
Implement AJAX with PHP
Implement Pagination for Database Records
Display Dynamic Content using MySQL Database
Display Recent Posts from Database
Implement Search Functionality
Implement Sort Functionality
Generate RSS Feed
Generate PDF File
Implement User Authentication
Implement User Authorization
Create Shopping Cart System
Implement Payment Gateway Integration
Create RESTful API using PHP
Implement Web Scraping
Implement Web Crawling
Display Weather Information
Create URL Shortener
Implement Role-Based Access Control (RBAC)
Create Chat Application
Create Todo List Application

Implement JWT (JSON Web Tokens) for Authentication

Create Blog System

Implement Multi-Language Support

Implement User Ratings and Reviews

Implement Image Gallery

Implement Google Maps Integration

Create Online Quiz System

Implement Data Encryption and Decryption

Create E-commerce Website

Implement Secure Password Storage

Implement Two-Factor Authentication

Hello World Program

```
<?php
echo "Hello, World!";
?>
```

Calculate Sum of Two Numbers

```
<?php
$num1 = 5;
$num2 = 10;
$sum = $num1 + $num2;
echo "Sum of $num1 and $num2 is: $sum";
?>
```

Check Even or Odd Number

```
<?php
$num = 6;
if ($num % 2 == 0) {
   echo "$num is even";
} else {
   echo "$num is odd";
}
?>
```

Find Factorial of a Number

```
<?php
$num = 5;
$factorial = 1;
for ($i = 1; $i <= $num; $i++) {
   $factorial *= $i;
}
echo "Factorial of $num is: $factorial";
```

```
?>
```

Check Prime Number

```
<?php
$num = 7;
$isPrime = true;
for ($i = 2; $i <= sqrt($num); $i++) {
    if ($num % $i == 0) {
        $isPrime = false;
        break;
    }
}
if ($isPrime) {
    echo "$num is prime";
} else {
    echo "$num is not prime";
}
?>
```

Reverse a String

```
<?php
$str = "Hello, World!";
$reverse = strrev($str);
echo "Original String: $str<br>";
echo "Reversed String: $reverse";
?>
```

Count Number of Words in a String

```
<?php
$str = "This is a sample sentence.";
$wordCount = str_word_count($str);
```

```
echo "Number of words in the string: $wordCount";
?>
```

Palindrome Check

```
<?php
$str = "madam";
$reverse = strrev($str);
if ($str == $reverse) {
   echo "$str is a palindrome";
} else {
   echo "$str is not a palindrome";
}
?>
```

Generate Fibonacci Series

```
<?php
$num = 10;
$first = 0;
$second = 1;
echo "Fibonacci Series up to $num terms:";
echo "$first, $second";
for ($i = 2; $i < $num; $i++) {
   $next = $first + $second;
   echo ", $next";
   $first = $second;
   $second = $next;
}
?>
```

Find Largest Number in an Array

```
<?php
$array = [5, 10, 3, 8, 2];
$largest = $array[0];
foreach ($array as $num) {
    if ($num > $largest) {
        $largest = $num;
    }
}
echo "Largest number in the array is: $largest";
?>
```

Find Smallest Number in an Array

```
<?php
$array = [5, 10, 3, 8, 2];
$smallest = $array[0];
foreach ($array as $num) {
    if ($num < $smallest) {
        $smallest = $num;
    }
}
echo "Smallest number in the array is: $smallest";
?>
```

Bubble Sort Algorithm

```
<?php
$array = [5, 10, 3, 8, 2];
$length = count($array);
for ($i = 0; $i < $length - 1; $i++) {
    for ($j = 0; $j < $length - $i - 1; $j++) {
        if ($array[$j] > $array[$j + 1]) {
```

```
            $temp = $array[$j];
            $array[$j] = $array[$j + 1];
            $array[$j + 1] = $temp;
        }
    }
}
echo "Sorted array using Bubble Sort: ";
foreach ($array as $num) {
    echo "$num ";
}
?>
```

Insertion Sort Algorithm

```
<?php
$array = [5, 10, 3, 8, 2];
$length = count($array);
for ($i = 1; $i < $length; $i++) {
    $key = $array[$i];
    $j = $i - 1;
    while ($j >= 0 && $array[$j] > $key) {
        $array[$j + 1] = $array[$j];
        $j = $j - 1;
    }
    $array[$j + 1] = $key;
}
echo "Sorted array using Insertion Sort: ";
foreach ($array as $num) {
    echo "$num ";
}
?>
```

Selection Sort Algorithm

```
<?php
$array = [5, 10, 3, 8, 2];
$length = count($array);
for ($i = 0; $i < $length - 1; $i++) {
    $min_index = $i;
    for ($j = $i + 1; $j < $length; $j++) {
        if ($array[$j] < $array[$min_index]) {
            $min_index = $j;
        }
    }
    $temp = $array[$i];
    $array[$i] = $array[$min_index];
    $array[$min_index] = $temp;
}
echo "Sorted array using Selection Sort: ";
foreach ($array as $num) {
    echo "$num ";
}
?>
```

Linear Search in an Array

```
<?php
$array = [5, 10, 3, 8, 2];
$search = 8;
$found = false;
foreach ($array as $index => $value) {
    if ($value == $search) {
        echo "Element $search found at index $index";
        $found = true;
        break;
```

```
    }
}
if (!$found) {
    echo "Element $search not found in the array";
}
?>
```

Binary Search Algorithm

```
<?php
function binarySearch($array, $search){
    $left = 0;
    $right = count($array) - 1;
    while ($left <= $right) {
        $mid = floor(($left + $right) / 2);
        if ($array[$mid] == $search) {
            return $mid;
        }
        if ($array[$mid] < $search) {
            $left = $mid + 1;
        } else {
            $right = $mid - 1;
        }
    }
    return -1;
}

$array = [2, 3, 5, 8, 10];
$search = 8;
$result = binarySearch($array, $search);
if ($result != -1) {
    echo "Element $search found at index $result";
```

```
} else {
    echo "Element $search not found in the array";
}
?>
```

Calculate Simple Interest

```
<?php
$principal = 1000;
$rate = 5;
$time = 2;
$simple_interest = ($principal * $rate * $time) / 100;
echo "Simple Interest: $simple_interest";
?>
```

Calculate Compound Interest

```
<?php
$principal = 1000;
$rate = 5;
$time = 2;
$compound_interest = $principal * (pow((1 + $rate / 100), $time)) - $principal;
echo "Compound Interest: $compound_interest";
?>
```

Generate Multiplication Table

```
<?php
$num = 5;
echo "Multiplication Table of $num:<br>";
for ($i = 1; $i <= 10; $i++) {
    echo "$num x $i = " . ($num * $i) . "<br>";
}
?>
```

Calculate Factorial Using Recursion

```
<?php
function factorial($num) {
   if ($num <= 1) {
      return 1;
   } else {
      return $num * factorial($num - 1);
   }
}
$num = 5;
echo "Factorial of $num is: " . factorial($num);
?>
```

Find GCD (Greatest Common Divisor)

```
<?php
function gcd($a, $b) {
   while ($b != 0) {
      $temp = $b;
      $b = $a % $b;
      $a = $temp;
   }
   return $a;
}
$num1 = 24;
$num2 = 36;
echo "GCD of $num1 and $num2 is: " . gcd($num1, $num2);
?>
```

Find LCM (Least Common Multiple)

```
<?php
function lcm($a, $b) {
    return ($a * $b) / gcd($a, $b);
}
function gcd($a, $b) {
    while ($b != 0) {
        $temp = $b;
        $b = $a % $b;
        $a = $temp;
    }
    return $a;
}
$num1 = 24;
$num2 = 36;
echo "LCM of $num1 and $num2 is: " . lcm($num1, $num2);
?>
```

Check Leap Year

```
<?php
$year = 2024;
if (($year % 4 == 0 && $year % 100 != 0) || ($year % 400 == 0)) {
    echo "$year is a leap year";
} else {
    echo "$year is not a leap year";
}
?>
```

Generate Random Numbers

```
<?php
$random_number = rand(1, 100);
```

```
echo "Random Number: $random_number";
?>
```

Generate Random Password

```
<?php
$password =
substr(str_shuffle('abcdefghijklmnopqrstuvwxyzABCDEFGHIJKLMNOPQRSTUVWX
YZ0123456789'), 0, 8);
echo "Random Password: $password";
?>
```

Calculate Area of a Circle

```
<?php
$radius = 5;
$area = M_PI * pow($radius, 2);
echo "Area of Circle: $area";
?>
```

Calculate Area of a Triangle

```
<?php
$base = 5;
$height = 8;
$area = 0.5 * $base * $height;
echo "Area of Triangle: $area";
?>
```

Calculate Area of a Rectangle

```
<?php
$length = 10;
$width = 5;
$area = $length * $width;
```

```
echo "Area of Rectangle: $area";
?>
```

Calculate Area of a Square

```
<?php
$side = 5;
$area = pow($side, 2);
echo "Area of Square: $area";
?>
```

Calculate Area of a Rhombus

```
<?php
$diagonal1 = 8;
$diagonal2 = 6;
$area = ($diagonal1 * $diagonal2) / 2;
echo "Area of Rhombus: $area";
?>
```

Calculate Area of a Trapezium

```
<?php
$base1 = 8;
$base2 = 6;
$height = 4;
$area = 0.5 * ($base1 + $base2) * $height;
echo "Area of Trapezium: $area";
?>
```

Calculate Volume of a Sphere

```
<?php
$radius = 5;
$volume = (4/3) * M_PI * pow($radius, 3);
```

```
echo "Volume of Sphere: $volume";
?>
```

Calculate Volume of a Cone

```
<?php
$radius = 5;
$height = 8;
$volume = (1/3) * M_PI * pow($radius, 2) * $height;
echo "Volume of Cone: $volume";
?>
```

Calculate Volume of a Cylinder

```
<?php
$radius = 5;
$height = 8;
$volume = M_PI * pow($radius, 2) * $height;
echo "Volume of Cylinder: $volume";
?>
```

Calculate Volume of a Cuboid

```
<?php
$length = 5;
$width = 4;
$height = 6;
$volume = $length * $width * $height;
echo "Volume of Cuboid: $volume";
?>
```

Convert Celsius to Fahrenheit

```
<?php
$celsius = 25;
```

```
$fahrenheit = ($celsius * 9/5) + 32;
echo "$celsius°C is equal to $fahrenheit°F";
?>
```

Convert Fahrenheit to Celsius

```
<?php
$fahrenheit = 77;
$celsius = ($fahrenheit - 32) * 5/9;
echo "$fahrenheit°F is equal to $celsius°C";
?>
```

Convert Kilometers to Miles

```
<?php
$kilometers = 10;
$miles = $kilometers * 0.621371;
echo "$kilometers kilometers is equal to $miles miles";
?>
```

Convert Miles to Kilometers

```
<?php
$miles = 6;
$kilometers = $miles * 1.60934;
echo "$miles miles is equal to $kilometers kilometers";
?>
```

Convert Decimal to Binary

```
<?php
$decimal = 10;
$binary = decbin($decimal);
echo "Binary representation of $decimal is: $binary";
?>
```

Convert Binary to Decimal

```
<?php
$binary = '1010';
$decimal = bindec($binary);
echo "Decimal representation of $binary is: $decimal";
?>
```

Convert Decimal to Octal

```
<?php
$decimal = 20;
$octal = decoct($decimal);
echo "Octal representation of $decimal is: $octal";
?>
```

Convert Octal to Decimal

```
<?php
$octal = '24';
$decimal = octdec($octal);
echo "Decimal representation of $octal is: $decimal";
?>
```

Convert Decimal to Hexadecimal

```
<?php
$decimal = 30;
$hexadecimal = dechex($decimal);
echo "Hexadecimal representation of $decimal is: $hexadecimal";
?>
```

Convert Hexadecimal to Decimal

```
<?php
$hexadecimal = '1E';
```

```
$decimal = hexdec($hexadecimal);
echo "Decimal representation of $hexadecimal is: $decimal";
?>
```

Generate a Simple Calculator

```
<?php
$num1 = 10;
$num2 = 5;
$operation = '+';
switch ($operation) {
    case '+':
        $result = $num1 + $num2;
        break;
    case '-':
        $result = $num1 - $num2;
        break;
    case '*':
        $result = $num1 * $num2;
        break;
    case '/':
        $result = $num1 / $num2;
        break;
    default:
        echo "Invalid operation";
        break;
}
echo "Result of $num1 $operation $num2 is: $result";
?>
```

Check Armstrong Number

```
<?php
$num = 153;
$temp = $num;
$sum = 0;
while ($temp != 0) {
  $remainder = $temp % 10;
  $sum += $remainder * $remainder * $remainder;
  $temp = (int)($temp / 10);
}
if ($num == $sum) {
  echo "$num is an Armstrong number";
} else {
  echo "$num is not an Armstrong number";
}
?>
```

Check Perfect Number

```
<?php
$num = 28;
$sum = 0;
for ($i = 1; $i <= $num / 2; $i++) {
  if ($num % $i == 0) {
    $sum += $i;
  }
}
if ($sum == $num) {
  echo "$num is a perfect number";
} else {
  echo "$num is not a perfect number";
}
```

```
?>
```

Display ASCII Value of a Character

```
<?php
$char = 'A';
$ascii = ord($char);
echo "ASCII value of $char is: $ascii";
?>
```

Generate a Calendar for a Month

```
<?php
$month = date('m');
$year = date('Y');
echo "Calendar for current month:<br>";
echo "<pre>";
echo `cal $month $year`;
echo "</pre>";
?>
```

Find Roots of a Quadratic Equation

```
<?php
$a = 1;
$b = -3;
$c = 2;
$delta = $b * $b - 4 * $a * $c;
if ($delta > 0) {
    $root1 = (-$b + sqrt($delta)) / (2 * $a);
    $root2 = (-$b - sqrt($delta)) / (2 * $a);
    echo "Roots of the quadratic equation are: $root1 and $root2";
} elseif ($delta == 0) {
    $root = -$b / (2 * $a);
```

```
    echo "Root of the quadratic equation is: $root";
} else {
    echo "Roots are imaginary";
}
?>
```

Implement Stack using Array

```
<?php
class Stack {
    private $stack;
        public function __construct() {
        $this->stack = [];
    }
    public function push($element) {
        array_push($this->stack, $element);
    }
    public function pop() {
        if (!$this->isEmpty()) {
            return array_pop($this->stack);
        }
        return null;
    }
    public function top() {
        if (!$this->isEmpty()) {
            return end($this->stack);
        }
        return null;
    }
    public function isEmpty() {
        return empty($this->stack);
    }
```

```
}
$stack = new Stack();
$stack->push(5);
$stack->push(10);
$stack->push(15);
echo "Top element of the stack: " . $stack->top() . "<br>";
echo "Popped element from the stack: " . $stack->pop() . "<br>";
echo "Top element of the stack after pop operation: " . $stack->top() . "<br>";
?>
```

Implement Queue using Array

```
<?php
class Queue {
    private $queue;

    public function __construct() {
        $this->queue = [];
    }

    public function enqueue($element) {
        array_push($this->queue, $element);
    }

    public function dequeue() {
        if (!$this->isEmpty()) {
            return array_shift($this->queue);
        }
        return null;
    }

    public function front() {
```

```
        if (!$this->isEmpty()) {
            return $this->queue[0];
        }
        return null;
    }

    public function isEmpty() {
        return empty($this->queue);
    }
}

$queue = new Queue();
$queue->enqueue(5);
$queue->enqueue(10);
$queue->enqueue(15);
echo "Front element of the queue: " . $queue->front() . "<br>";
echo "Dequeued element from the queue: " . $queue->dequeue() . "<br>";
echo "Front element of the queue after dequeue operation: " . $queue->front() . "<br>";
?>
```

Implement Singly Linked List

```
<?php
class Node {
    public $data;
    public $next;

    public function __construct($data) {
        $this->data = $data;
        $this->next = null;
    }
}
```

```
class SinglyLinkedList {
    private $head;

    public function __construct() {
        $this->head = null;
    }

    public function insert($data) {
        $newNode = new Node($data);
        if ($this->head === null) {
            $this->head = $newNode;
        } else {
            $current = $this->head;
            while ($current->next !== null) {
                $current = $current->next;
            }
            $current->next = $newNode;
        }
    }

    public function display() {
        $current = $this->head;
        while ($current !== null) {
            echo $current->data . " -> ";
            $current = $current->next;
        }
        echo "null";
    }
}
```

```
$list = new SinglyLinkedList();
$list->insert(5);
$list->insert(10);
$list->insert(15);
echo "Singly Linked List: ";
$list->display();
?>
```

Implement Doubly Linked List

```
<?php
class Node {
    public $data;
    public $prev;
    public $next;

    public function __construct($data) {
        $this->data = $data;
        $this->prev = null;
        $this->next = null;
    }
}

class DoublyLinkedList {
    private $head;
    private $tail;

    public function __construct() {
        $this->head = null;
        $this->tail = null;
    }
```

```
    public function insert($data) {
        $newNode = new Node($data);
        if ($this->head === null) {
            $this->head = $newNode;
            $this->tail = $newNode;
        } else {
            $newNode->prev = $this->tail;
            $this->tail->next = $newNode;
            $this->tail = $newNode;
        }
    }

    public function display() {
        $current = $this->head;
        while ($current !== null) {
            echo $current->data . " <-> ";
            $current = $current->next;
        }
        echo "null";
    }
}

$list = new DoublyLinkedList();
$list->insert(5);
$list->insert(10);
$list->insert(15);
echo "Doubly Linked List: ";
$list->display();
?>
```

Implement Circular Linked List

```
<?php
class Node {
    public $data;
    public $next;

    public function __construct($data) {
        $this->data = $data;
        $this->next = null;
    }
}

class CircularLinkedList {
    private $head;

    public function __construct() {
        $this->head = null;
    }

    public function insert($data) {
        $newNode = new Node($data);
        if ($this->head === null) {
            $this->head = $newNode;
            $newNode->next = $this->head;
        } else {
            $current = $this->head;
            while ($current->next !== $this->head) {
                $current = $current->next;
            }
            $current->next = $newNode;
            $newNode->next = $this->head;
```

```
        }
    }

    public function display() {
        $current = $this->head;
        do {
            echo $current->data . " -> ";
            $current = $current->next;
        } while ($current !== $this->head);
        echo "head";
    }
}

$list = new CircularLinkedList();
$list->insert(5);
$list->insert(10);
$list->insert(15);
echo "Circular Linked List: ";
$list->display();
?>
```

Implement Binary Search Tree (BST)

```
<?php
class Node {
    public $data;
    public $left;
    public $right;

    public function __construct($data) {
        $this->data = $data;
        $this->left = null;
```

```
        $this->right = null;
    }
}

class BinarySearchTree {
    private $root;

    public function __construct() {
        $this->root = null;
    }

    public function insert($data) {
        $newNode = new Node($data);
        if ($this->root === null) {
            $this->root = $newNode;
        } else {
            $current = $this->root;
            while (true) {
                if ($data < $current->data) {
                    if ($current->left === null) {
                        $current->left = $newNode;
                        break;
                    } else {
                        $current = $current->left;
                    }
                } else {
                    if ($current->right === null) {
                        $current->right = $newNode;
                        break;
                    } else {
                        $current = $current->right;
```

```
                    }
                }
            }
        }
    }

    public function displayInOrder($node) {
        if ($node !== null) {
            $this->displayInOrder($node->left);
            echo $node->data . " ";
            $this->displayInOrder($node->right);
        }
    }
}

$bst = new BinarySearchTree();
$bst->insert(50);
$bst->insert(30);
$bst->insert(70);
$bst->insert(20);
$bst->insert(40);
echo "In-order traversal of BST: ";
$bst->displayInOrder($bst->root);
?>
```

Implement Insertion Sort Algorithm

```
<?php
function insertionSort($array) {
    $length = count($array);
    for ($i = 1; $i < $length; $i++) {
        $key = $array[$i];
```

```
        $j = $i - 1;
        while ($j >= 0 && $array[$j] > $key) {
            $array[$j + 1] = $array[$j];
            $j = $j - 1;
        }
        $array[$j + 1] = $key;
    }
    return $array;
}

$array = [5, 10, 3, 8, 2];
echo "Sorted array using Insertion Sort: ";
print_r(insertionSort($array));
?>
```

Implement Merge Sort Algorithm

```
<?php
function merge($left, $right) {
    $result = [];
    $leftLength = count($left);
    $rightLength = count($right);
    $i = $j = 0;
    while ($i < $leftLength && $j < $rightLength) {
        if ($left[$i] < $right[$j]) {
            $result[] = $left[$i];
            $i++;
        } else {
            $result[] = $right[$j];
            $j++;
        }
    }
```

```
    while ($i < $leftLength) {
        $result[] = $left[$i];
        $i++;
    }
    while ($j < $rightLength) {
        $result[] = $right[$j];
        $j++;
    }
    return $result;
}

function mergeSort($array) {
    $length = count($array);
    if ($length <= 1) {
        return $array;
    }
    $mid = (int)($length / 2);
    $left = mergeSort(array_slice($array, 0, $mid));
    $right = mergeSort(array_slice($array, $mid));
    return merge($left, $right);
}

$array = [5, 10, 3, 8, 2];
echo "Sorted array using Merge Sort: ";
print_r(mergeSort($array));
?>
```

Implement Quick Sort Algorithm

```
<?php
function quickSort($array) {
    $length = count($array);
```

```
    if ($length <= 1) {
        return $array;
    }
    $pivot = $array[0];
    $left = $right = [];
    for ($i = 1; $i < $length; $i++) {
        if ($array[$i] < $pivot) {
            $left[] = $array[$i];
        } else {
            $right[] = $array[$i];
        }
    }
    return array_merge(quickSort($left), [$pivot], quickSort($right));
}

$array = [5, 10, 3, 8, 2];
echo "Sorted array using Quick Sort: ";
print_r(quickSort($array));
?>
```

Generate Pascal's Triangle

```
<?php
function generatePascalsTriangle($rows) {
    $triangle = [];
    for ($i = 0; $i < $rows; $i++) {
        $triangle[$i] = [];
        for ($j = 0; $j <= $i; $j++) {
            if ($j == 0 || $j == $i) {
                $triangle[$i][$j] = 1;
            } else {
                $triangle[$i][$j] = $triangle[$i - 1][$j - 1] + $triangle[$i - 1][$j];
```

```
            }
        }
    }
    return $triangle;
}

$rows = 5;
$pascalsTriangle = generatePascalsTriangle($rows);
echo "Pascal's Triangle:<br>";
foreach ($pascalsTriangle as $row) {
    echo implode(" ", $row) . "<br>";
}
?>
```

Validate Email Address

```
<?php
$email = "example@example.com";
if (filter_var($email, FILTER_VALIDATE_EMAIL)) {
    echo "$email is a valid email address";
} else {
    echo "$email is not a valid email address";
}
?>
```

Send Email using PHP

```
<?php
$to = "recipient@example.com";
$subject = "Test Email";
$message = "This is a test email.";
$headers = "From: sender@example.com";
if (mail($to, $subject, $message, $headers)) {
```

```
    echo "Email sent successfully";
} else {
    echo "Failed to send email";
}
?>
```

Create Login System

```
<?php
session_start();
if (isset($_POST['login'])) {
    $username = "example";
    $password = "password";
    if ($_POST['username'] == $username && $_POST['password'] == $password) {
        $_SESSION['username'] = $username;
        header("Location: welcome.php");
        exit;
    } else {
        echo "Invalid username or password";
    }
}
?>
<!DOCTYPE html>
<html>
<head>
    <title>Login</title>
</head>
<body>
    <h2>Login</h2>
    <form method="post" action="">
        <label>Username:</label>
        <input type="text" name="username" required><br>
```

```
        <label>Password:</label>
        <input type="password" name="password" required><br>
        <button type="submit" name="login">Login</button>
    </form>
</body>
</html>
```

Create Registration Form

```
<?php
if (isset($_POST['register'])) {
    $username = $_POST['username'];
    $email = $_POST['email'];
    $password = $_POST['password'];
    // Perform registration process here
    echo "Registration successful!";
}
?>
<!DOCTYPE html>
<html>
<head>
    <title>Registration</title>
</head>
<body>
    <h2>Registration</h2>
    <form method="post" action="">
        <label>Username:</label>
        <input type="text" name="username" required><br>
        <label>Email:</label>
        <input type="email" name="email" required><br>
        <label>Password:</label>
        <input type="password" name="password" required><br>
```

```
    <button type="submit" name="register">Register</button>
  </form>
</body>
</html>
```

File Upload and Validation

```
<?php
if (isset($_POST['upload'])) {
  $targetDir = "uploads/";
  $targetFile = $targetDir . basename($_FILES['file']['name']);
  $fileType = pathinfo($targetFile, PATHINFO_EXTENSION);
  $allowedTypes = ['jpg', 'jpeg', 'png', 'gif'];
  if (in_array($fileType, $allowedTypes)) {
    if (move_uploaded_file($_FILES['file']['tmp_name'], $targetFile)) {
      echo "File uploaded successfully";
    } else {
      echo "Error uploading file";
    }
  } else {
    echo "Invalid file type";
  }
}
?>
<!DOCTYPE html>
<html>
<head>
  <title>File Upload</title>
</head>
<body>
  <h2>File Upload</h2>
  <form method="post" action="" enctype="multipart/form-data">
```

```
    <input type="file" name="file" required><br>
    <button type="submit" name="upload">Upload</button>
  </form>
</body>
</html>
```

File Download Script

```
<?php
$file = "example.txt";
if (file_exists($file)) {
  header('Content-Description: File Transfer');
  header('Content-Type: application/octet-stream');
  header('Content-Disposition: attachment; filename=' . basename($file));
  header('Content-Length: ' . filesize($file));
  readfile($file);
} else {
  echo "File not found";
}
?>
```

Create Simple CMS (Content Management System)

```
<?php
session_start();
if (!isset($_SESSION['username'])) {
  header("Location: login.php");
  exit;
}
$content = "";
if ($_SERVER['REQUEST_METHOD'] == 'POST') {
  $content = $_POST['content'];
  file_put_contents("content.txt", $content);
```

```
    echo "Content saved successfully!";
} else {
    $content = file_get_contents("content.txt");
}
?>
<!DOCTYPE html>
<html>
<head>
    <title>Simple CMS</title>
</head>
<body>
    <h2>Edit Content</h2>
    <form method="post" action="">
        <textarea name="content" rows="10" cols="50"><?php echo $content;
?></textarea><br>
        <button type="submit">Save</button>
    </form>
</body>
</html>
```

Generate XML File using PHP

```
<?php
$xml = new DOMDocument();
$xml->formatOutput = true;
$root = $xml->createElement("books");
$xml->appendChild($root);

$book1 = $xml->createElement("book");
$title1 = $xml->createElement("title", "Book 1");
$author1 = $xml->createElement("author", "Author 1");
$book1->appendChild($title1);
```

```
$book1->appendChild($author1);
$root->appendChild($book1);

$book2 = $xml->createElement("book");
$title2 = $xml->createElement("title", "Book 2");
$author2 = $xml->createElement("author", "Author 2");
$book2->appendChild($title2);
$book2->appendChild($author2);
$root->appendChild($book2);

$xml->save("books.xml");
echo "XML file generated successfully!";
?>
```

Parse XML File using PHP

```
<?php
$xml = simplexml_load_file("books.xml");
echo "Books:<br>";
foreach ($xml->book as $book) {
    echo "Title: " . $book->title . ", Author: " . $book->author . "<br>";
}
?>
```

Create JSON Response using PHP

```
<?php
$response = [
    "name" => "John Doe",
    "age" => 30,
    "email" => "john@example.com"
];
echo json_encode($response);
```

```
?>
```

Parse JSON Data using PHP

```
<?php
$jsonString = '{"name": "John", "age": 30, "city": "New York"}';
$data = json_decode($jsonString, true);
echo "Name: " . $data['name'] . ", Age: " . $data['age'] . ", City: " . $data['city'];
?>
```

Implement CRUD Operations (Create, Read, Update, Delete)

```
<?php
// Database connection
$servername = "localhost";
$username = "username";
$password = "password";
$dbname = "users";

$conn = new mysqli($servername, $username, $password, $dbname);

// Check connection
if ($conn->connect_error) {
   die("Connection failed: " . $conn->connect_error);
}

// Create operation
if (isset($_POST['create'])) {
   $username = $_POST['username'];
   $email = $_POST['email'];
   $password = $_POST['password'];
```

```
    $sql = "INSERT INTO users (username, email, password) VALUES ('$username',
'$email', '$password')";

    if ($conn->query($sql) === TRUE) {
        echo "New record created successfully";
    } else {
        echo "Error: " . $sql . "<br>" . $conn->error;
    }
}

// Read operation
$sql = "SELECT * FROM users";
$result = $conn->query($sql);

if ($result->num_rows > 0) {
    echo "<h2>User List</h2>";
    echo "<table border='1'><tr><th>ID</th><th>Username</th><th>Email</th></tr>";
    while ($row = $result->fetch_assoc()) {
        echo "<tr><td>" . $row["id"] . "</td><td>" . $row["username"] . "</td><td>" .
$row["email"] . "</td></tr>";
    }
    echo "</table>";
} else {
    echo "0 results";
}

// Update operation
if (isset($_POST['update'])) {
    $id = $_POST['id'];
    $username = $_POST['username'];
    $email = $_POST['email'];
```

```
    $sql = "UPDATE users SET username='$username', email='$email' WHERE id=$id";

    if ($conn->query($sql) === TRUE) {
        echo "Record updated successfully";
    } else {
        echo "Error updating record: " . $conn->error;
    }
}

// Delete operation
if (isset($_POST['delete'])) {
    $id = $_POST['id'];

    $sql = "DELETE FROM users WHERE id=$id";

    if ($conn->query($sql) === TRUE) {
        echo "Record deleted successfully";
    } else {
        echo "Error deleting record: " . $conn->error;
    }
}

// Close connection
$conn->close();
?>

<!DOCTYPE html>
<html>
<head>
    <title>User Management</title>
```

```
</head>
<body>
    <h2>Add New User</h2>
    <form method="post" action="">
        <label>Username:</label>
        <input type="text" name="username" required><br>
        <label>Email:</label>
        <input type="email" name="email" required><br>
        <label>Password:</label>
        <input type="password" name="password" required><br>
        <button type="submit" name="create">Create</button>
    </form>

    <h2>Update User</h2>
    <form method="post" action="">
        <label>ID:</label>
        <input type="number" name="id" required><br>
        <label>New Username:</label>
        <input type="text" name="username" required><br>
        <label>New Email:</label>
        <input type="email" name="email" required><br>
        <button type="submit" name="update">Update</button>
    </form>

    <h2>Delete User</h2>
    <form method="post" action="">
        <label>ID:</label>
        <input type="number" name="id" required><br>
        <button type="submit" name="delete">Delete</button>
    </form>
</body>
```

```
</html>
```

Generate Captcha Image

```
<?php
session_start();
$randomString =
substr(str_shuffle("0123456789abcdefghijklmnopqrstuvwxyzABCDEFGHIJKLMNOP
QRSTUVWXYZ"), 0, 5);
$_SESSION['captcha'] = $randomString;
$image = imagecreate(100, 40);
$bgColor = imagecolorallocate($image, 255, 255, 255);
$textColor = imagecolorallocate($image, 0, 0, 0);
imagestring($image, 5, 20, 12, $randomString, $textColor);
header("Content-type: image/png");
imagepng($image);
imagedestroy($image);
?>
```

Implement Image Upload and Resize

```
<?php
if (isset($_POST['upload'])) {
   $targetDir = "uploads/";
   $targetFile = $targetDir . basename($_FILES['file']['name']);
   move_uploaded_file($_FILES['file']['tmp_name'], $targetFile);
   echo "File uploaded successfully";
}

?>
<!DOCTYPE html>
<html>
<head>
```

```
    <title>Image Upload</title>
</head>
<body>
    <h2>Upload Image</h2>
    <form method="post" action="" enctype="multipart/form-data">
        <input type="file" name="file" required><br>
        <button type="submit" name="upload">Upload</button>
    </form>
</body>
</html>
```

Generate Thumbnails of Images

php

Copy code

```
<?php
$sourceFile = "image.jpg";
$destinationFile = "thumbnail.jpg";
list($width, $height) = getimagesize($sourceFile);
$newWidth = 100;
$newHeight = ($height / $width) * $newWidth;
$source = imagecreatefromjpeg($sourceFile);
$destination = imagecreatetruecolor($newWidth, $newHeight);
imagecopyresized($destination, $source, 0, 0, 0, 0, $newWidth, $newHeight, $width,
$height);
imagejpeg($destination, $destinationFile);
echo "Thumbnail generated successfully";
?>
```

Implement AJAX with PHP

```
<?php
if (isset($_GET['name'])) {
```

```
  echo "Hello, " . $_GET['name'] . "!";
}
?>
<!DOCTYPE html>
<html>
<head>
  <title>AJAX Example</title>
  <script>
    function greet() {
      var name = document.getElementById("name").value;
      var xhr = new XMLHttpRequest();
      xhr.onreadystatechange = function() {
        if (xhr.readyState == 4 && xhr.status == 200) {
          document.getElementById("result").innerHTML = xhr.responseText;
        }
      };
      xhr.open("GET", "ajax.php?name=" + name, true);
      xhr.send();
    }
  </script>
</head>
<body>
  <h2>Greeting</h2>
  <input type="text" id="name">
  <button onclick="greet()">Greet</button>
  <div id="result"></div>
</body>
</html>
```

Implement Pagination for Database Records

```
<?php
// Database connection
$servername = "localhost";
$username = "username";
$password = "password";
$dbname = "mydatabase";

$conn = new mysqli($servername, $username, $password, $dbname);

// Check connection
if ($conn->connect_error) {
    die("Connection failed: " . $conn->connect_error);
}

// Pagination variables
$limit = 5; // Number of records per page
$page = isset($_GET['page']) ? $_GET['page'] : 1; // Current page number
$start = ($page - 1) * $limit; // Starting limit for records

// Query to fetch records with pagination
$sql = "SELECT * FROM your_table LIMIT $start, $limit";
$result = $conn->query($sql);

// Fetch total number of records
$total_records_query = "SELECT COUNT(*) as total FROM your_table";
$total_records_result = $conn->query($total_records_query);
$total_records = $total_records_result->fetch_assoc()['total'];

// Calculate total number of pages
$total_pages = ceil($total_records / $limit);
```

```
// Display records
if ($result->num_rows > 0) {
   echo "<h2>Records</h2>";
   echo "<table border='1'><tr><th>ID</th><th>Name</th></tr>";
   while ($row = $result->fetch_assoc()) {
      echo "<tr><td>" . $row["id"] . "</td><td>" . $row["name"] . "</td></tr>";
   }
   echo "</table>";
} else {
   echo "No records found";
}

// Pagination links
echo "<br>";
echo "<ul>";
for ($i = 1; $i <= $total_pages; $i++) {
   echo "<li><a href='pagination.php?page=" . $i . "'>" . $i . "</a></li>";
}
echo "</ul>";

// Close connection
$conn->close();
?>
```

Display Dynamic Content using MySQL Database

```
<?php
// Database connection
$servername = "localhost";
$username = "username";
$password = "password";
```

```
$dbname = "mydatabase";

$conn = new mysqli($servername, $username, $password, $dbname);

// Check connection
if ($conn->connect_error) {
   die("Connection failed: " . $conn->connect_error);
}

// Query to fetch dynamic content from database
$sql = "SELECT * FROM dynamic_content";
$result = $conn->query($sql);

// Display content
if ($result->num_rows > 0) {
   echo "<h2>Dynamic Content</h2>";
   while ($row = $result->fetch_assoc()) {
      echo "<h3>" . $row["title"] . "</h3>";
      echo "<p>" . $row["content"] . "</p>";
   }
} else {
   echo "No content found";
}

// Close connection
$conn->close();
?>
```

Display Recent Posts from Database

```
<?php
// Database connection
$servername = "localhost";
$username = "username";
$password = "password";
$dbname = "mydatabase";

$conn = new mysqli($servername, $username, $password, $dbname);

// Check connection
if ($conn->connect_error) {
    die("Connection failed: " . $conn->connect_error);
}

// Query to fetch recent posts from database
$sql = "SELECT * FROM posts ORDER BY created_at DESC LIMIT 5"; // Fetch 5
most recent posts
$result = $conn->query($sql);

// Display recent posts
if ($result->num_rows > 0) {
    echo "<h2>Recent Posts</h2>";
    while ($row = $result->fetch_assoc()) {
        echo "<h3>" . $row["title"] . "</h3>";
        echo "<p>" . $row["content"] . "</p>";
        echo "<p><strong>Posted on:</strong> " . $row["created_at"] . "</p>";
    }
} else {
    echo "No posts found";
}
```

```
// Close connection
$conn->close();
?>
```

Implement Search Functionality

```
<!DOCTYPE html>
<html lang="en">
<head>
   <meta charset="UTF-8">
   <meta name="viewport" content="width=device-width, initial-scale=1.0">
   <title>Search Page</title>
</head>
<body>
   <h2>Search Page</h2>
   <form method="get" action="">
      <input type="text" name="query" placeholder="Enter your search query" required>
      <button type="submit">Search</button>
   </form>
   <hr>

   <?php
   // Database connection
   $servername = "localhost";
   $username = "username";
   $password = "password";
   $dbname = "mydatabase";

   $conn = new mysqli($servername, $username, $password, $dbname);

   // Check connection
```

```
    if ($conn->connect_error) {
        die("Connection failed: " . $conn->connect_error);
    }

    // Process search query
    if (isset($_GET['query'])) {
        $search_query = $_GET['query'];

        // Query to search for records in the database
        $sql = "SELECT * FROM your_table WHERE title LIKE '%$search_query%' OR
content LIKE '%$search_query%'";
        $result = $conn->query($sql);

        // Display search results
        if ($result->num_rows > 0) {
            echo "<h3>Search Results:</h3>";
            while ($row = $result->fetch_assoc()) {
                echo "<h4>" . $row["title"] . "</h4>";
                echo "<p>" . $row["content"] . "</p>";
            }
        } else {
            echo "<p>No results found.</p>";
        }
    }

    // Close connection
    $conn->close();
    ?>
</body>
</html>
```

Implement Sort Functionality

```
<?php
// Array of numbers to be sorted
$numbers = [5, 2, 8, 1, 3];

// Sort in ascending order
sort($numbers);

// Print sorted array
echo "Sorted array in ascending order: ";
foreach ($numbers as $num) {
    echo $num . " ";
}

echo "<br>";

// Sort in descending order
rsort($numbers);

// Print sorted array
echo "Sorted array in descending order: ";
foreach ($numbers as $num) {
    echo $num . " ";
}
?>
```

Generate RSS Feed

```
<?php
header("Content-Type: application/rss+xml; charset=UTF-8");
```

```
echo "<?xml version='1.0' encoding='UTF-8'?>";
echo "<rss version='2.0'>";
echo "<channel>";
echo "<title>My RSS Feed</title>";
echo "<link>https://example.com</link>";
echo "<description>This is a sample RSS feed.</description>";

// Assuming $items is an array of items to be included in the feed
foreach ($items as $item) {
  echo "<item>";
  echo "<title>" . $item['title'] . "</title>";
  echo "<description>" . $item['description'] . "</description>";
  echo "<link>" . $item['link'] . "</link>";
  echo "</item>";
}

echo "</channel>";
echo "</rss>";
?>
```

Generate PDF File

```
<?php
require('fpdf.php'); // Include FPDF library

$pdf = new FPDF();
$pdf->AddPage();
$pdf->SetFont('Arial', '', 12);
$pdf->Cell(0, 10, 'Hello, World!', 0, 1, 'C');
$pdf->Output('example.pdf', 'D'); // Output the PDF as a download
?>
```

Implement User Authentication

```
<?php
session_start();

if (isset($_POST['login'])) {
    $username = $_POST['username'];
    $password = $_POST['password'];

    // Validate username and password from database
    if ($username == 'admin' && $password == 'admin123') {
        $_SESSION['username'] = $username;
        header('Location: dashboard.php');
        exit;
    } else {
        echo "Invalid username or password";
    }
}
?>
<!DOCTYPE html>
<html>
<head>
    <title>Login</title>
</head>
<body>
    <h2>Login</h2>
    <form method="post" action="">
        <label>Username:</label>
        <input type="text" name="username" required><br>
        <label>Password:</label>
        <input type="password" name="password" required><br>
        <button type="submit" name="login">Login</button>
```

```
  </form>
</body>
</html>
```

Implement User Authorization

```
<?php
session_start();

// Check if user is logged in and authorized
if (!isset($_SESSION['username'])) {
   header('Location: login.php');
   exit;
}

// Check user's role or permissions to access certain pages or perform actions
if ($_SESSION['role'] != 'admin') {
   echo "You are not authorized to access this page";
   exit;
}
?>
```

Create Shopping Cart System

```
<?php
session_start();
// Add item to cart
if (isset($_POST['add_to_cart'])) {
   $product_id = $_POST['product_id'];
   $quantity = $_POST['quantity'];

   // Add item to cart array
   $_SESSION['cart'][$product_id] = $quantity;
```

```
    echo "Item added to cart successfully";
}

// Remove item from cart
if (isset($_GET['remove_from_cart'])) {
    $product_id = $_GET['remove_from_cart'];

    // Remove item from cart array
    unset($_SESSION['cart'][$product_id]);

    echo "Item removed from cart successfully";
}

// Clear cart
if (isset($_GET['clear_cart'])) {
    // Clear cart array
    $_SESSION['cart'] = array();

    echo "Cart cleared successfully";
}
?>
```

Implement Payment Gateway Integration

```
<?php
// Code for integrating with a payment gateway would depend on the specific gateway being used, and typically involves sending data to the gateway's API and handling the response. Below is a basic example:

if (isset($_POST['checkout'])) {
    $total_amount = $_POST['total_amount'];
```

```
    $gateway_url = 'https://example.com/payment'; // Gateway's URL
    $post_data = array(
        'total_amount' => $total_amount,
        // Other required parameters for the payment
    );

    // Send data to the payment gateway using cURL
    $ch = curl_init();
    curl_setopt($ch, CURLOPT_URL, $gateway_url);
    curl_setopt($ch, CURLOPT_POST, 1);
    curl_setopt($ch, CURLOPT_POSTFIELDS, http_build_query($post_data));
    curl_setopt($ch, CURLOPT_RETURNTRANSFER, true);
    $response = curl_exec($ch);
    curl_close($ch);

    // Process response from the payment gateway
    if ($response === false) {
        echo "Error processing payment";
    } else {
        // Handle payment response
        echo "Payment processed successfully";
    }
}
?>
```

Create RESTful API using PHP

```
<?php
// Sample RESTful API implementation using PHP

// Set headers to allow cross-origin resource sharing (CORS)
header("Access-Control-Allow-Origin: *");
```

```
header("Content-Type: application/json; charset=UTF-8");

// Check request method
if ($_SERVER['REQUEST_METHOD'] === 'GET') {
    // Return some sample data
    $data = array(
        "message" => "This is a sample response from the RESTful API",
        "timestamp" => time()
    );

    // Encode data to JSON format
    echo json_encode($data);
} else {
    // If method is not GET, return error message
    http_response_code(405); // Method Not Allowed
    echo json_encode(array("error" => "Method not allowed"));
}
?>
```

Implement Web Scraping

```
<?php
// Sample web scraping implementation using PHP

// Load HTML content from a URL
$html = file_get_contents('https://example.com');

// Extract specific data using DOMDocument
$dom = new DOMDocument();
@$dom->loadHTML($html);
$titles = $dom->getElementsByTagName('title');
```

```
// Get title of the webpage
$title = $titles->item(0)->nodeValue;

// Output title
echo "Title of the webpage: " . $title;
?>
```

Implement Web Crawling

```
<?php
// Sample web crawling implementation using PHP

// Function to crawl a webpage
function crawl($url) {
  $html = file_get_contents($url);

  // Extract links using regular expression
  preg_match_all('/<a href="([^"]+)"/', $html, $matches);
  $links = $matches[1];

  // Output crawled links
  echo "Crawled links from $url:<br>";
  foreach ($links as $link) {
    echo "<a href='$link'>$link</a><br>";
  }
}

// Call crawl function with a starting URL
crawl('https://example.com');
?>
```

Display Weather Information

```php
<?php
// Sample weather information display using PHP

// Sample API endpoint for weather data
$api_url =
'https://api.openweathermap.org/data/2.5/weather?q=London&appid=YOUR_API_KEY
';

// Get weather data from the API
$weather_data = file_get_contents($api_url);

// Decode JSON data
$weather_info = json_decode($weather_data);

// Extract relevant information
$city = $weather_info->name;
$temperature = $weather_info->main->temp;
$description = $weather_info->weather[0]->description;

// Output weather information
echo "Weather in $city: $description, Temperature: $temperature";
?>
```

Create URL Shortener

```php
<?php
// Sample URL shortener implementation using PHP

// Function to generate a random short code
function generateShortCode($length = 6) {
```

```
    $chars =
'0123456789abcdefghijklmnopqrstuvwxyzABCDEFGHIJKLMNOPQRSTUVWXYZ';
    $code = '';
    for ($i = 0; $i < $length; $i++) {
        $code .= $chars[rand(0, strlen($chars) - 1)];
    }
    return $code;
}

// Sample URL to be shortened
$url = 'https://example.com/page';

// Generate short code
$short_code = generateShortCode();

// Save short code and original URL in a database or file
// For demonstration purposes, we'll just output the shortened URL
$shortened_url = "https://short.url/$short_code";

// Output shortened URL
echo "Shortened URL: $shortened_url";
?>
```

Implement Role-Based Access Control (RBAC)

php

Copy code

```
<?php
// RBAC implementation example
// For demonstration purposes, we'll define roles and check access based on the role of the user
```

```
// Define user roles
$roles = array(
    'admin' => array('create', 'read', 'update', 'delete'),
    'user' => array('read')
);

// Check access for a user based on their role and requested action
function checkAccess($role, $action) {
    global $roles;
    if (isset($roles[$role]) && in_array($action, $roles[$role])) {
        return true;
    } else {
        return false;
    }
}

// Example usage
$userRole = 'admin';
$action = 'delete';
if (checkAccess($userRole, $action)) {
    echo "User has access to perform $action action.";
} else {
    echo "User does not have access to perform $action action.";
}
?>
```

Create Chat Application

```
<?php
// Chat application implementation example
// This example demonstrates a simple chat application using PHP and AJAX
```

```
// Chat log file
$logFile = 'chat_log.txt';

// Function to get chat log
function getChatLog() {
   global $logFile;
   return file_get_contents($logFile);
}

// Function to save chat message
function saveMessage($message) {
   global $logFile;
   file_put_contents($logFile, $message . PHP_EOL, FILE_APPEND | LOCK_EX);
}

// Check if message is submitted
if (isset($_POST['message'])) {
   $message = $_POST['message'];
   saveMessage($message);
   echo "Message sent successfully!";
}

// Display chat log
echo "<h2>Chat Log</h2>";
echo "<div id='chatLog'>" . getChatLog() . "</div>";
?>

<!-- Chat form -->
<form id="chatForm" method="post" action="">
   <input type="text" name="message" placeholder="Type your message here..."
required>
```

```
    <button type="submit">Send</button>
</form>

<!-- AJAX script to update chat log without page reload -->
<script>
    setInterval(function() {
        $('#chatLog').load('chat.php #chatLog');
    }, 1000);
</script>
```

Create Todo List Application

```
<?php
// Todo list application implementation example
// This example demonstrates a simple todo list application using PHP and MySQL

// Database connection
$servername = "localhost";
$username = "username";
$password = "password";
$dbname = "todo_app";

$conn = new mysqli($servername, $username, $password, $dbname);

// Check connection
if ($conn->connect_error) {
    die("Connection failed: " . $conn->connect_error);
}

// Fetch todo list from database
$sql = "SELECT * FROM todos";
$result = $conn->query($sql);
```

```
// Display todo list
if ($result->num_rows > 0) {
    echo "<h2>Todo List</h2>";
    echo "<ul>";
    while ($row = $result->fetch_assoc()) {
        echo "<li>" . $row["task"] . "</li>";
    }
    echo "</ul>";
} else {
    echo "No tasks found";
}

// Close connection
$conn->close();
?>
```

Implement JWT (JSON Web Tokens) for Authentication

```
<?php
// JWT authentication implementation example
// This example demonstrates how to generate and verify JWT tokens for authentication

// Include the library for JWT (e.g., firebase/php-jwt)
require 'vendor/autoload.php';

use Firebase\JWT\JWT;

// Secret key for JWT
$secret_key = 'YOUR_SECRET_KEY';

// User data for authentication
```

```
$userData = array(
    'user_id' => 123,
    'username' => 'example_user'
);

// Generate JWT token
$jwt_token = JWT::encode($userData, $secret_key);

// Decode and verify JWT token
try {
    $decoded = JWT::decode($jwt_token, $secret_key, array('HS256'));
    print_r($decoded);
} catch (Exception $e) {
    echo 'Error: ' . $e->getMessage();
}
?>
```

Create Blog System

```
<?php
// Blog system implementation example
// This example demonstrates a simple blog system using PHP and MySQL

// Database connection
$servername = "localhost";
$username = "username";
$password = "password";
$dbname = "blog_db";

$conn = new mysqli($servername, $username, $password, $dbname);

// Check connection
```

```
if ($conn->connect_error) {
    die("Connection failed: " . $conn->connect_error);
}

// Fetch blog posts from database
$sql = "SELECT * FROM posts";
$result = $conn->query($sql);

// Display blog posts
if ($result->num_rows > 0) {
    echo "<h2>Blog Posts</h2>";
    while ($row = $result->fetch_assoc()) {
        echo "<h3>" . $row["title"] . "</h3>";
        echo "<p>" . $row["content"] . "</p>";
    }
} else {
    echo "No posts found";
}

// Close connection
$conn->close();
?>
```

Implement Multi-Language Support

```
<?php
// Multi-language support implementation example
// This example demonstrates how to implement multi-language support in PHP

// Default language
$default_language = 'en';
```

```
// Get preferred language from request or user settings
$user_language = isset($_GET['lang']) ? $_GET['lang'] : $default_language;

// Load language file based on user's preferred language
require_once "lang/{$user_language}.php";

// Example usage
echo $lang['welcome_message'];
?>
```

Implement User Ratings and Reviews

```
<?php
// User ratings and reviews implementation example
// This example demonstrates how to implement user ratings and reviews in PHP and
MySQL

// Database connection
$servername = "localhost";
$username = "username";
$password = "password";
$dbname = "ratings_db";

$conn = new mysqli($servername, $username, $password, $dbname);

// Check connection
if ($conn->connect_error) {
    die("Connection failed: " . $conn->connect_error);
}

// Fetch user ratings and reviews from database
$sql = "SELECT * FROM ratings";
```

```
$result = $conn->query($sql);

// Display user ratings and reviews
if ($result->num_rows > 0) {
   echo "<h2>User Ratings and Reviews</h2>";
   while ($row = $result->fetch_assoc()) {
      echo "<p>Rating: " . $row["rating"] . "</p>";
      echo "<p>Review: " . $row["review"] . "</p>";
   }
} else {
   echo "No ratings and reviews found";
}

// Close connection
$conn->close();
?>
```

Implement Image Gallery

```
<?php
// Image Gallery implementation example
// This example demonstrates how to create a simple image gallery using PHP

// Array of image URLs
$images = array(
   "image1.jpg",
   "image2.jpg",
   "image3.jpg"
);
// Display images
echo "<h2>Image Gallery</h2>";
echo "<div class='gallery'>";
```

```
foreach ($images as $image) {
    echo "<img src='$image' alt='Image'>";
}
echo "</div>";
?>
```

Implement Google Maps Integration

```
<!DOCTYPE html>
<html>
<head>
    <title>Google Maps Integration</title>
    <!-- Include Google Maps API -->
    <script
src="https://maps.googleapis.com/maps/api/js?key=YOUR_API_KEY"></script>
    <style>
        /* Set the size of the map */
        #map {
            height: 400px;
            width: 100%;
        }
    </style>
</head>
<body>
    <h2>Google Maps Integration</h2>
    <!-- Display Google Map -->
    <div id="map"></div>

    <script>
        // Initialize the map
        function initMap() {
            // Define the location
```

```
        var location = {lat: 40.7128, lng: -74.0060}; // Example: New York City
coordinates

        // Create a map object and specify the DOM element for display.
        var map = new google.maps.Map(document.getElementById('map'), {
          center: location,
          zoom: 12 // Set the initial zoom level
        });

        // Create a marker and set its position
        var marker = new google.maps.Marker({
          map: map,
          position: location,
          title: 'Marker Title' // Optional: Add a title to the marker
        });
    }
  </script>

  <!-- Load the map after the page has fully loaded -->
  <script async defer
src="https://maps.googleapis.com/maps/api/js?key=YOUR_API_KEY&callback=initM
ap"></script>
</body>
</html>
```

Create Online Quiz System

Database Structure

```
CREATE TABLE questions (
  id INT AUTO_INCREMENT PRIMARY KEY,
  question_text TEXT NOT NULL
);
```

```
CREATE TABLE options (
   id INT AUTO_INCREMENT PRIMARY KEY,
   question_id INT,
   option_text VARCHAR(255) NOT NULL,
   is_correct TINYINT(1) DEFAULT 0,
   FOREIGN KEY (question_id) REFERENCES questions(id)
);
```

HTML Form (quiz.php)

```
<!DOCTYPE html>
<html>
<head>
   <title>Online Quiz</title>
</head>
<body>
   <h2>Online Quiz</h2>
   <form method="post" action="quiz_submit.php">
      <?php
      // Connect to the database
      $conn = new mysqli("localhost", "username", "password", "quiz_db");
      // Check connection
      if ($conn->connect_error) {
         die("Connection failed: " . $conn->connect_error);
      }
      // Fetch questions from the database
      $sql = "SELECT * FROM questions";
      $result = $conn->query($sql);
      // Display questions and options
      if ($result->num_rows > 0) {
         $question_number = 1;
         while ($row = $result->fetch_assoc()) {
```

```
            echo "<p><strong>Question $question_number:</strong>
{$row['question_text']}</p>";
            // Fetch options for the current question
            $options_sql = "SELECT * FROM options WHERE question_id =
{$row['id']}";
            $options_result = $conn->query($options_sql);

            // Display options as radio buttons
            while ($option_row = $options_result->fetch_assoc()) {
              echo "<input type='radio' name='question{$row['id']}'
value='{$option_row['id']}'> {$option_row['option_text']}<br>";
            }
            $question_number++;
          }
      } else {
          echo "No questions found.";
      }
      $conn->close();
      ?>
      <br>
      <button type="submit">Submit</button>
   </form>
</body>
</html>
```

PHP Script to Handle Quiz Submission (quiz_submit.php)

```
<?php
// Connect to the database
$conn = new mysqli("localhost", "username", "password", "quiz_db");

// Check connection
if ($conn->connect_error) {
```

```
    die("Connection failed: " . $conn->connect_error);
}

// Initialize variables
$score = 0;
$total_questions = 0;

// Loop through each submitted answer
foreach ($_POST as $question_id => $selected_option_id) {
    // Fetch correct option for the current question
    $sql = "SELECT is_correct FROM options WHERE id = $selected_option_id";
    $result = $conn->query($sql);
    if ($result->num_rows > 0) {
        $row = $result->fetch_assoc();
        if ($row['is_correct'] == 1) {
            $score++; // Increment score if the selected option is correct
        }
        $total_questions++;
    }
}

// Calculate percentage score
$percentage_score = ($score / $total_questions) * 100;

// Display quiz result
echo "<h2>Quiz Result</h2>";
echo "<p>Your Score: $score / $total_questions</p>";
echo "<p>Percentage Score: $percentage_score%</p>";

$conn->close();
?>
```

Implement Data Encryption and Decryption

```
<?php
// Function to encrypt data
function encryptData($data, $key, $iv) {
  // Encrypt the data using AES encryption algorithm
  $encrypted_data = openssl_encrypt($data, 'AES-256-CBC', $key, 0, $iv);
  return $encrypted_data;
}
// Function to decrypt data
function decryptData($encrypted_data, $key, $iv) {
  // Decrypt the data using AES decryption algorithm
  $decrypted_data = openssl_decrypt($encrypted_data, 'AES-256-CBC', $key, 0, $iv);
  return $decrypted_data;
}

// Main code
$data = "Hello, world!";
$key = "your_secret_key"; // Should be a 32-character string for AES-256-CBC
encryption
$iv = openssl_random_pseudo_bytes(16); // Generate random IV (Initialization Vector)

// Encrypt data
$encrypted_data = encryptData($data, $key, $iv);
echo "Encrypted Data: $encrypted_data\n";

// Decrypt data
$decrypted_data = decryptData($encrypted_data, $key, $iv);
echo "Decrypted Data: $decrypted_data\n";

?>
```

Create E-commerce Website

Database Structure (MySQL)

```
CREATE TABLE products (
    id INT AUTO_INCREMENT PRIMARY KEY,
    name VARCHAR(100) NOT NULL,
    price DECIMAL(10, 2) NOT NULL,
    description TEXT
);
```

product.php (Display Products)

```
<!DOCTYPE html>
<html lang="en">
<head>
    <meta charset="UTF-8">
    <meta name="viewport" content="width=device-width, initial-scale=1.0">
    <title>Product List</title>
    <style>
        .product {
            border: 1px solid #ccc;
            border-radius: 5px;
            padding: 10px;
            margin: 10px;
            width: 300px;
            float: left;
        }
    </style>
</head>
<body>
    <h2>Product List</h2>
    <div class="products">
        <?php
```

```
    // Connect to database
    $conn = new mysqli("localhost", "username", "password", "ecommerce_db");

    // Check connection
    if ($conn->connect_error) {
      die("Connection failed: " . $conn->connect_error);
    }

    // Fetch products from database
    $sql = "SELECT * FROM products";
    $result = $conn->query($sql);

    // Display products
    if ($result->num_rows > 0) {
      while ($row = $result->fetch_assoc()) {
        echo "<div class='product'>";
        echo "<h3>{$row['name']}</h3>";
        echo "<p>{$row['description']}</p>";
        echo "<p>Price: {$row['price']}</p>";
        echo "</div>";
      }
    } else {
      echo "No products found.";
    }

    // Close connection
    $conn->close();
    ?>
  </div>
</body>
</html>
```

Implement Secure Password Storage

```php
<?php
// Function to securely hash a password
function hashPassword($password) {
    $hashed_password = password_hash($password, PASSWORD_DEFAULT);
    return $hashed_password;
}

// Function to verify a password against its hashed version
function verifyPassword($password, $hashed_password) {
    return password_verify($password, $hashed_password);
}

// Example usage
$password = "password123";
$hashed_password = hashPassword($password);

// Verify password
if (verifyPassword($password, $hashed_password)) {
    echo "Password is correct";
} else {
    echo "Password is incorrect";
}

?>
```

Implement Two-Factor Authentication

```
{
    "require": {
        "phpgangsta/googleauthenticator": "^2.0"
```

```
    }
}
```

After creating the composer.json file, run the following command in your terminal to install the library:

composer install

Two-Factor Authentication Program:

php

Copy code

```php
<?php
require_once 'vendor/autoload.php';

use PHPGangsta\GoogleAuthenticator\GoogleAuthenticator;

// Function to generate a random secret key
function generateSecretKey() {
    $ga = new GoogleAuthenticator();
    return $ga->createSecret();
}

// Function to generate a QR code URL for the given secret key and user name
function generateQRCodeUrl($userName, $secretKey) {
    $ga = new GoogleAuthenticator();
    return $ga->getQRCodeGoogleUrl($userName, $secretKey);
}

// Function to verify the provided token against the secret key
function verifyToken($secretKey, $token) {
    $ga = new GoogleAuthenticator();
    return $ga->verifyCode($secretKey, $token);
}
```

```
// Example usage

// Generate a secret key for the user
$secretKey = generateSecretKey();

// Generate a QR code URL for the user to scan
$userName = 'JohnDoe';
$qrCodeUrl = generateQRCodeUrl($userName, $secretKey);

echo "Scan the QR code below using the Google Authenticator app:\n";
echo "<img src='$qrCodeUrl' alt='QR Code'><br>";

// Simulate the user entering the token generated by the Google Authenticator app
$token = '123456'; // Example token

// Verify the token
if (verifyToken($secretKey, $token)) {
    echo "Token is valid. Two-factor authentication successful.\n";
} else {
    echo "Token is invalid. Two-factor authentication failed.\n";
}

?>
```

www.ingramcontent.com/pod-product-compliance
Lightning Source LLC
LaVergne TN
LVHW052052160826
845678LV00015B/3185

* 9 7 8 9 3 3 4 0 6 5 5 6 5 *